THOSE RIGID MUSINGS

UDAISA RAINA

ISBN 978-1-68494-224-4

*"**Those Rigid Musings**" is a sum of all the musings of not only me but of all the human hearts and the purpose of this book is to give you a glimpse of ups and downs of the emotions which collide over every heart beat and also somehow make you realize that sufferings are common to all, it's not only me or you who is suffering and fortunate are those who find their own delight and live their lives to the fullest.*

Happy roller coaster ride!

Contents

Contents

Preface

It was a harsh winter day when I was done with everything, palpitating, a pen in my hand, scratched a paper that turned out to be a beautiful pattern and realized that there is always a way through every hardship that will lead us forget our agony. At that time I wrote a poem and since then I never felt that I'm done with writing. I wrote everything that bothered me as I've always felt that I've been a misunderstood creature who acts immature no matter what. In the aura of nobody understanding me and everyone only suggesting and advising things, I was in a need of a listener that no body was ready to be. I found in paper a partner who would listen to me and in pen a partner who would help me narrated my emotions. Through writing I got to know that it's ok to not be fine and we don't need to fake it at all.

I was born in a male dominated society and am always been told to act like an ideal girl but I defied to be one. I neither am nor would want to be an ideal girl according to the vision of this 'society.' Not only this thing, I used to muse over other issues as well, in fact I get still get mused over things. That is when I decided to collect my musings and that is how "Those Rigid Musings" came into being.

I know, I'm not the only one who is suffering from problems like family issues, trust issues, getting abandoned etc. And that is when I thought of publishing my musings because in one way or the another, everyone would relate to it.

People, especially girls don't face only said problems. There are alot of problems that we come across in our lives which us make their prey.

I want 'us' to oppose the evils like harassment, sex discrimination, molestation etc. First I thought of not mentioning the same in my musings because of the fear of being an evil but realized that it's high time for me to take and initiative that might help alot of people in taking a stand for themselves.

I can proudly say that not only once but more than once I always stood tall before this and I chose to become a survivor rather than a victim. This thing has become a major musing for me.

Digital Distribution.

Publishing-in-support-of,

sarafali.in

The voice of unpublished writings.

Mohalla Sultanpura, opp partap exclusive hostel Wali Gali, main stop Janipur, Jammu - 180007

Facebook : Saraf Ali Bhat | sarafali101@gmail.com

---

*Book published and managed on digital stores by **sarafali.in***

1. Grudges

I've never been one to hold a grudge;
Holding it is not easy like eating a fudge,
Thinking about it causes all the smudge,
And people think it's nothing but a nudge.
Mostly I remain in pique,
And all the way want to shriek, Maybe because I'm not aware of
the technique,
Of how to be on peak.
Ahhh! I wish my life could be surrounded by the mystique.

2. Break The Taboo

Let's talk about periods,
Oh no! we will sound like idiots,
It's more like forbidden,
And by this I am sicken.
Can't talk about rape either,
Because talks like these should be underneath her,
She is not allowed to speak,
And this sounds like a foolish freak.
From all this nonsense I want to be free,
And that is how a writer developed in me,
Let's speak being away from the stickiness of this glue,
And be real humans by 'breaking this taboo.'

3. Tears

What do tears symbolize? Sometimes pain of a mother, When
her child is in pain.
Sometimes sadness of a brother,
When her sister is about to leave him.
Sometimes guilt of a child,
Who made his parents sad.
Sometimes worriness of a father,
When her daughter doesn't return on time.
Sometimes gladness of a student,
Who topped the exam even being a backbencher.
Sometimes, somewhere, somehow,
Tears may symbolise a lot more!

4. I Wonder!

How have I transformed, I wonder.
Is it good or bad, I wonder.
Before, why did I feel flustered, I wonder.
Why did I pretend to be elated, I wonder.
Now, how have I gained that ingenuity, I wonder.
How was the journey of getting evolved, I wonder.
But why do people find it mundane, I wonder.
Further, why do 'I' get affected, I wonder!

5. That Lovely Night

That night, when my vision was wan,
I was feeling like a corpse, But still was alive.
Looking at the spilling stars,
Doze and pale, which seemed.
Like them, I also felt ashen.
Just wanted to cry, The tears of blood. The brightness of the
moon,
Wanted to wither me grey.
That night, which was pushing me to infirmity,
Which was leading to the loss of generosity,
That night, which tried to meet reality.
That night was harsh and lonely.

6. I See Myself In.........

I see myself in her colored dupatta,
Which poured there whole colours in my life.
In her chattering bangles,
Making the sound of my first foot steps.
Also in her shringhar,
Showing me a glimpse of my future. Someday, someone will also
see herself in me,
So,I also see myself in me.

7. Why?

I know you love me,
So why can't you stop being dominant?
If you don't want to see me sad,
Then why don't you make me happy? You know that I love to
enjoy my youngness,
So why are you making these days older?
When my life is pretty much bright,
With your anger, why do you make it dark?
Even though I have a father,
Then why do I feel abandoned?

8. Track Of Imagination

I want to go to the place,
Where the sky and earth meet.
Even after knowing,
Horizon is just an illusion.
I want to sleep in the lap of that aura,
When evening prepares to meet night.
Even after knowing,
It's just a beautiful confusion.
I want to live the moment,
When clouds caste their shadow on me.
Even after knowing,
It's just a paradigm of deceit.

9. The Vision Of Love

I want to love,
I want to care.
In the air like the dove,
From the world who doesn't fear.
In your arms is where I belong,
Away from the world of deception.
Want to spend my life long,
Without being in the fear of corruption.
Currently I'm missing you,
Missing the time, we today lack.
Ohhhh beloved I really do,
Can you please come back?

10. Voice Of Your Child

Do you think it's right?
In front of your kids, you guys fight.
They want to stop you but they don't dare,
Because you have anyway put them in fear.
I swear, your kids get hurt, By all this disgusting dirt.
By your fights, they get affected,
And somehow their future gets defected.
Your children definitely don't get good,
Because you don't do, what you should.
To their ills, be the cure,
By being your better version, for sure.

11. Vanishing Kashmir

There is a place in the world, Which is considered as gold.
But today it isn't the same,
Thanks to all those people,
Who are playing a dirty game.
Kashmir!, has now became a hell, But once it was a heaven as
well. There is a strange thing that I've found,
Kashmiris are in fear, all around.
In the heart of every mother, there is a flood of tears, Will her son
return home?, every mother fears. It's not easy for a father to put
his son in coffin,
And women become widows, very often.
People are oppressed and we call it democracy, But what
happens, is more like hypocrisy.
Whatever 'real' happens is actually 'fake'.
Can't all this be stopped, for god's sake?

12. Patterns Of Life

Everybody want success,
But nobody wants to work. Everybody want good relations, But
nobody stops back biting.
Everybody want happiness,
But nobody wants to earn it. Everybody wants understandings,
But nobody understands others.
Everybody want perfection, But nobody stops criticism.
Everybody want to change all this,
But nobody does the same.

13. You Are Unbelievable

Why do you want to impress?
And put yourself in stress.
Despite of you don't show,
By putting up your eyebrow.
A person should have bank balance,
Doesn't matter if it will lead to some violence.
It sounds more than funny,
When people say, everything is money.
People will definitely get jealous,
By showing them, you didn't get less.
You anyhow do flaunt,
Perhaps, that is what you want!

14. Difference Exists

Not all men want women as servants.
Not all women want money all the time.
Not all children consider parents as a burden.
Not all boys want to rule over girls.
Not all parents love their son more.
Not all teachers make education a business.
Not all people understand, some are different.

15. Pages Of An Unseen Book

Trust me, I got totally hooked, To an old book, when I looked.
I saw a spark in her eyes, which today has faiden,
Ya, it was an album of a lady, when she was a maiden.
Some pages, of a girl who was sassy,
And who would do anything to be classy.
In some pages, I could see her springtime with changing caliber.
Due to struggle, the next page developed in to a rupture.
Second last page of a sad women, from her father's house who was pulled up,
After marriage she had kids and her heart became filled up.
She accepts all the tantrums and with 'his' anger has to contend.
She is a mother and therefore, this last page will never have an end.

16. Themeless Writing

I have nothing to say, But I want to write. Don't know about
what,
But I want to write.
Right now, my brain is blank But I want to write. My thoughts
are completely frozen,
But I want to write.
I feel like I've spoken about everything,
But I want to write. All words seem to be quite,
But I want to write.
There is no more ink in my pen, But I want to write.
Maybe with my blood,
But I want to write

17. Time To Realize

You cheat your family, don't you feel so,
You are on a wrong track, where you are not suppose to go.
Okay! so by this you are addicted
But if you continue this, your future can't be predicted.
Miserable will be, by this your life,
You should remember the vows with your wife.
You promised her father to be with her all time,
And for your children's sake, stop making this crime.
I know, you are in a doubt,
And wondering, what am I talking about. Smoking! Is
something which is not wise,
I know you know, it's time to realize.

18. Where is Where?

Where everyone speak of the doldrums,
Where your loved ones let you be in agony,
Where the aura is always jittled,
Where there are yields of negativity,
Where people make 'me' a delusive me,
Where life is an unsolved puzzle,
Where where is everywhere!

19. Soul Full Of Wishes

I wish the world stops;
When my mother smiles, When my brother says, "you look
beautiful."
When my father encourages me.
I wish to be the strongest;
When I hold the pen,
When people underestimate me,
When I think of making the world better.
I wish this all could happen;
When I can't find happiness,
When I loose my self belief
When I think, I'm done.

20. Mirror Reflections

Looking in the mirror,
What so you see?, A glint of disappointment,
Of a person locked and lost his key.
Lips struggling with,
That continuous fake smile.
Eyes struggling with , Those pity hopes.
Ears struggling with,
Extremely rude coments.
Body struggling with,
The soul less life.
Looking in the mirror,
What do you see?, A glint of disappointment,
Of a person locked and lost his key.

21. Golden Memories

To an old wall, I looked,

Those golden memories were still hooked.

In some ugly, but,

Meaningful pits and digs.

Captured are by pits, The slogans of joy.

Perceived are by the digs,

Different colours of peace.

Today I have nothing to do, With either the wall or memories.

But I don't know.

Of what do I fear!

Maybe because I know, That the memories will blow.

From these beautifully ugly walls.

And maybe from my mind and heart too.

22. Once Upon A Time

Yesterday I looked at her,
She brought the colour of hard work, with the sunrise.
The colour of passion, with the noon.
The colour of joy, with the sunset.
The colour of hope, with the cycles of moon.
Today, I again looked at her.
Rays of the sun seemed ill.
Sun in the noontime was tired.
Sun was ashen at sunset.
And moon acted like a corpse.

23. Compassion Error

Yeah, she wrought everything,

She is pious and modest,

Okay, she procured a lot of strength,

She is a Master of exactitude,

Wow, she is an ecumenical icon,

Undoubtedly there is a huge difference between her and I;

'I' am 'I' and 'she' is 'she.'

24. Grown Up Parents

Ya, I do seem quizzical,

Because all this is at odds. They are not allowed to do their
defence,

And according to you, it makes sense.

Everyone can't be a doctor, Nor can everyone be great.

At sometimes, some are good,

And some are great in maintaining brotherhood.

Why do you force them to be what you want, And expect them to
do the same.

And when they do what they want instead,

It doesn't fit your head and ask them to find their own bread.

Learn to move along with time,

And stop being lucid about their future.

Because time can't move along with you.

And understand, if they'll be happy, you will be too.

25. From 'I' and 'Him'

I am when done and full of sleep,
I dream of your eyes and your shadows deep,
Then on you, I think of writing a book,
But realize, I still can't explain the effects of that one look.
You did a miracle, by adding in me that special grace.
That comes with nothing but the way you embrace the smile on
your face.
There is much more special other than the smile on you,
Which I've always loved with love, ya, that's true.
Alike you, you made me a star.
And gave me the brightness, brighter than the brightest glowing
bar.
Explaining your brightness may lead to the lack of ink.
And to forever feel that, my eyes don't even blink.

26. Candle

Every drop of the wax,
That pours from the candle,
Tells me to speak
If the words are still mine. Every flame of the candle,
Which is sprinted outwards,
Tells me to look far,
If my eyes are not covered.
Every candle which is burnt,
But still has a space,
Tells me to be alive,
Even after death.

27. It Is Something

From the very beginning,
I have always been told,
It is nothing You can't buy by it, happiness, On the streets of Lal
Chowk. You can't succeed by it, in life,
Like a miracle full of miracles.
And from the very beginning,
I have been observing, If it is something. You can buy the things,
That make you happy. You can do the things,
That will succeed you in life.
Ya, MONEY is not everything
But, ' it is something.'

28. It's Fine

It's fine to feel low, It's fine to ignore it.
It's fine to recall your past.
It's fine to have mixed feelings.
It's fine to feel alone in the crowd.
It's fine to be quizzical.
It's fine to have a smile behind a crying soul.
It's fine to hide emotions.
It's fine to be fine!

29. This & That

To be 'that' elated,
I want resurrect 'this' dead within myself.
Just want to yield 'that' illumination,
From 'this' unwanted delusiveness.
In search of 'that' vigor, In 'this' odious world.
To that 'that', I wish to reach,
From this unwanted 'this.'

30. Out Of My Mind!

What is the most difficult thing?
To get in, into yourself.
And to let you know,
If you are actually alive.
To find your soul,
Which belongs to your body.
To make your brain,
Aware of your heart.
To be aware of the fact,
That your heart doesn't beat for you.
To make yourself believe, That life is a metaphor.

31. Flaws Are Flawless

I am a moon, full of spots, But I still look gorgeous. I make your
nights brighter, And your soul lighter.
Then why do I get neglected?,
If I'm there for you in the day as well.
Of course, because something more bright brightens up your day.
There are times, when I look flawless,
And there are times when others look flawless.
Ya, it's just about the perfect time,
Otherwise every flaw is flawless.

32. Speak The Unspoken

There is alot to speak,
That has made us weak.
While we upload pictures with using the best filter,
Some are still struggling to find a shelter.
Dark people are considered are dull,
But it's actually your mind which is null.
People have forgotten humanity, And run after fame.
Without realising that it's actually lame.
Today, in this world there is all around blood,
But without uttering even a word, people remain in this flood.
Ya, everything I spoke about left us broken,
But, there is still alot unspoken.

33. Desires

I want to care for someone,
Just like a mother cares for her child.
I want to enjoy every moment, Just like a crazy hedonist.
I want to feel forever young,
Just like the snowfall of Kashmir. I want to be free from
oppression,
Just like a martyr after death.
I want to calm and glad,
Just like the lovers in the moonlight.
I want to live life with a zest.
Just like a writer writes his desires.

34. Mystery

Everything seems to be blurry,
Every time in the state of jittery,
Struggling to find out if I'm worthy, To be under the lord's
mercy.
It's tough to find out a prosperous journey,
Which will lead me to the world of Hillary,
Yeah, I find everything a big mystery.

35. Chaotic World

Most of the people are imperious,
Always urging to be deleterious,
Some are also mysterious,
Every time, about everything, people become serious.
For all the people including me, Happiness is demotic.
It seems illegal like narcotic.
Even tough with life we can also develop a relationship which is
symbiotic,
But still, we tend to make everything chaotic.

36. Feel The Pain

Do we feel the pain?
Of the beggers begging in the cold.
Of people sleeping without food.
Of children wandering without clothes.
Can't we stop doing this show off?
And look around instead.
To give little sympathy.
And help the needy.
Why this partiality?
On the basis of fair and dark.
Don't know if we do or not.
But one should definitely feel the pain.

37. Love?

About love, I have always over mused,
Whenever I think about it I still get confused.
I loved to sit on the window and gaze, And never wanted to miss
that phase.
Through the streets, whenever I used to walk,
I always missed the way he talk.
Love can't be defined with a word,
It can only be compared to a flying bird.
I would do anything to not make him sad, But instead he
treated me like I was mad.
I would always cry in the light which is dim,
But then I realized, I get nothing by remembering him.
This part of my life, I wish could get cropped, And fine happiness
that indeed I've dropped.
If Love actually isn't what I mentioned above,
Then I want to know, what is Love?

38. SHE

She can no longer endure the brunt.
For her, 'it's all my aunt.' She chose to see good in others,
And ended up finding good in herself.
For 'this', she can't waste her strength.
They can keep theirs as well.
If she weeps in the sky, she can fly as well.
She always aimed the moon, and even if she failed,
She landed amongst the stars. Her pen and paper made her
gorgeous, And at the end, she found herself.

39. It Starts With You

Look around you, you will find everyone sad,
Because whatever happens, happens bad.
This is what people always think.
But nobody knows what will happen in the next blink.
Good times will definitely happen, maybe late, So, stop cursing
your fate.
From a terrible tsunami to a house which is burnt,
What happens has something new, that you haven't learnt.
Full of negativity, if you wear a shroud, All seems to be the
same,in the crowd. Where you find everyday, everywhere noise,
But if you observe, thier might be alot wise.
You should notice, whenever the breeze blows, Like the moon,
your skin glows.
So stop behaving like someone who is mad.
And enjoy each and every moment like a child.
In life, learn to flow like a kite,
And I'm sure, you'll find your own delight.
Like alot of people did, you can do it too, Just remember it all
starts with you.

Printed by Libri Plureos GmbH in Hamburg,
Germany